BipQuiz

100 QUESTIONS & ANSWERS

Animals

Illustrations by Florence MacKenzie

Sterling Publishing Co., Inc. New York

10 9 8 7 6 5 4 3 2 1
Published by Sterling Publishing Company, Inc.
387 Park Avenue South, New York, N.Y. 10016
© 1994 by InfoMedia Communication
English translation © 1994 by Sterling Publishing Co., Inc.
Distributed in Canada by Sterling Publishing
% Canadian Manda Group, P.O. Box 920, Station U
Toronto, Ontario, Canada M8Z 5P9
Printed and bound in Italy
All rights reserved
Sterling ISBN 0-8069-0933-1

BipQuiz

100 QUESTIONS & ANSWERS

Animals

How to Use the BipPen

The BipPen must be held straight to point to the black dot.

Point to a black dot.

A continuous sound (beeeep) and a red light mean that you've chosen the wrong answer.

Point to a black dot.

A discontinuous sound (beep beep beep) and a green light mean that you've chosen the right answer.

Keep your BipPen for our other books.

Headings

Each question belongs to a specific heading.
Each heading is identified by a color.

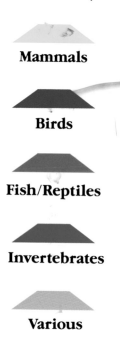

Mammals

Birds

Fish/Reptiles

Invertebrates

Various

1

Animals are divided into two main
categories: invertebrates (no backbone)
and:

vertebrates
fish
mollusks

2

The species name designates a group of
animals which can reproduce with each
other. Members of the same species may live
in different parts of the world. How many
species are there?

over 500,000
over 1 million
over 2 million

Carnivorous animals eat meat and herbivorous animals graze on grass or eat bush and tree leaves. To which group does the rhinoceros belong?

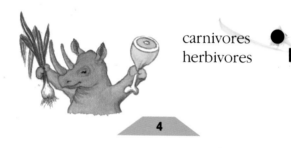

carnivores ●
herbivores ■

Carnivores are predators, which means that they attack live animals to eat their flesh or to suck on their blood. What are their victims called?

grazers ●
flesh-eating ■
prey ▲

Felines are carnivorous mammals. Except for one feline, all have retractable claws. This one, which is also the fastest in the world at 65 mph (110 km/hr), is the:

bear
cheetah
house cat

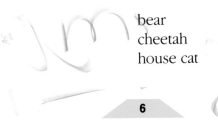

The brown bear lives in wild mountain forests. It eats everything, but it especially loves honey and raspberries. It lives in:

a burrow
a nest
a den

Farm animals; including hens, ducks and geese, are kept inside at night for their own protection. Rabbits, which are more excitable, are kept in:

nurseries
hutches
stalls

Wolves travel in packs. Each pack has an order of dominance, so that each animal knows whom it must obey. The pack leader is called the:

alpha
beta
head

All 80 whale species are mammals whose hearts can weigh up to a ton. The biggest whale's total weight can be 190 tons and it can measure up to 100 ft. (30 m). It is the:

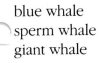

blue whale
sperm whale
giant whale

Eagles are found throughout the world. They have strong claws with which to catch prey. These claws are called:

talons
stilts
legs

Turtles seem to hold the record for longevity: One was given to the king of the Tonga archipelago in 1773 and the turtle died in an accident in 1966. Unlike that of other reptiles, its body is protected by:

armor
shield
shell

Insects are six-legged winged invertebrates that form their own class. Eight-legged invertebrates form the arachnid class. Which animal belongs to it?

fish
spider
mouse

S ome animals hunt by day (diurnal),
while others hunt by night (nocturnal).
The bat, for example, is nocturnal. The bat is
the only mammal to:

fly
suck blood
eat vegetables

B irds of prey have curved beaks and
powerful claws; they eat small animals
that they can see from the sky. Which of
these three is not a bird of prey?

vulture
eagle
starling

With the coming of winter, some animals sleep until spring after having abundantly fed. This sleep is called:

fattening up
hibernating
dreaming

Cows produce milk to feed their calves. Thus a cow must give birth in order to give the farmer her milk. After each birth, a cow produces milk for approximately:

10 years
2 months
1 year

S ome birds (storks), mammals (elephants), and fish (tuna) change location with the seasons. What is this called?

migration
great trip
eternal return

F reshwater turtles live in rivers and ponds, but sometimes they climb onto dry land to warm themselves, and because the sun:

lets them breathe
colors their shell
hardens their shell

Amphibians are born in water but live mostly on dry land as adults. This is true of:

frogs
slugs
woodcocks

Of the 250 shark species, 25 are dangerous to man. A shark's five rows of teeth are replaced when they fall out. In 10 years, a tiger shark loses as many as:

10,000 teeth
20,000 teeth
1000 teeth

An elephant absorbs ⅕ of its weight in food each day and drinks approximately 200 quarts (litres) of water. How much water can it absorb in a single drink?

1 quart ●

9 quarts ■

100 quarts ▲

Giraffes must sleep standing up, or they wouldn't be able to get themselves back up again. There are two types on the African continent: the giraffe and the okapi. The okapi lives in the forest. Where does the giraffe live?

in the jungle ●

in the savannah ■

in the tundra ▲

G orillas live in groups of 16 to 30 individuals, composed of females, offspring, and one male. They live in patches of forest and sleep in:

nests
caves
burrows

P olar bears can swallow *almost* anything but unless they're starving, they principally feed only on a few parts of the seal. Which parts?

liver and heart
kidneys and lungs
fat and intestines

Birds' feathers help them fly as well as protect them from the cold. This is why aquatic birds have more feathers than do other birds. Swans have:

5000 to 10,000
900 to 1000
20,000 to 30,000

To fight other males, deer grow these weapons on their heads. These weapons fall off each winter and grow back each spring. They're called:

antlers
ears
tusks

Zebras belong to the same genus as horses and donkeys. Zebras are lions' favorite prey; they're rarely attacked by any animals other than lions. Zebras live exclusively in:

America ●

Asia ■

Africa ▲

Horses can be divided into two large groups: saddle horses, ridden by man, and draft horses that do diverse tasks. An example of a draft horse is:

an Arabian ●

a Percheron ■

a mule ▲

Birds regularly replace their old feathers with new ones. This transformation occurs during periods of relative inactivity and is called:

falling
transferring
molting

Gorillas are the largest apes. An adult male can measure 5′9″ (1.75 m) and weigh 440 lbs. (200 kgs). Gorillas are herbivores and have no natural enemies. What is their average life span?

5 years
35 years
100 years

I f you catch a lizard by its tail, the tail falls off so that the lizard can escape. This is a defensive reflex. The tail:

grows back in a day ●
grows back in several months ■
never grows back ▲

C rickets chirp by rubbing their hind legs against their wings. They do so more loudly than usual when:

rain is coming ●
the temperature rises ■
the temperature falls ▲

The cobra, one of the most dangerous snakes in the world, is found in Asia and Africa. Its venom kills within a period from 15 minutes to 6 hours. In India it is also known as the monocled snake, where it kills an average of:

50 people per year
10,000 people per year
1000 people per year

All animals adapt to their environment. In burning deserts, some can go without drinking for a few weeks. This is true of:

the dromedary
the elephant
the giraffe

The oceans have the largest number and greatest variety of animals, from microscopic plankton to the giant whale. Oceans account for what percentage of the earth's surface?

70%
10%
99%

Ants (10,000 species) live in highly organized colonies. Some ants, known as soldiers, protect the community, while others tend to the queen. These "tenders" are known as:

servants
workers
assistants

A spider secretes a silk thread from its abdomen. This silk thread is stronger than steel wire, and, when woven into a web, lets the spider:

capture insects
shelter itself from the rain
play on the trampoline

Monkeys feed on vegetable matter (nuts, fruits), and sometimes on eggs and insects. One of them also eats meat. Which one?

gorilla
chimpanzee
orangutan

S ome ants mark trails that lead to food using a chemical product they produce themselves, and which only attracts ants of the same species. A teaspoon of this product can mark trails ranging over:

62 miles (100 km)
620 miles (1000 km)
937,500 miles
(1,500,000 km)

M any animals use camouflage to hide from their enemies. Bitterns imitate reeds, stretching their bodies and pointing their beaks to the sky. They even rock when the wind is blowing. They live:

on the seashore
in the forest
in marshes

K oalas rarely come down from trees; they only eat the leaves of some varieties of eucalyptus. They live in:

Australia
Italy
Scandinavia

T here are almost 900 bird species in the world. These are divided into various categories (aquatic birds, birds of prey . . .), but they all have feathers and lay eggs. Which is the biggest bird in the world?

the heron
the ostrich
the crane

Lions are felines that live in families of 6 to 20 individuals. They feed on zebra and antelope and sometimes on carrion. Hunting is an activity reserved for:

males ●
females ■
both ▲

The slowest of all mammals, the sloth, lives in trees and only rarely comes down to the ground, where it crawls with some difficulty. To cover 0.625 mile (1 km) a sloth needs:

10 minutes ●
2 days ■
6 hours ▲

The Ganges River dolphin lives in India's sacred river. Like other dolphins, it uses an ultrasound emission system both to orient itself and to find food. Why is it unique?

it's purple
it's tiny
it's blind

Some animals lose their brown summer fur or feathers and grow a white coat for winter, allowing them to remain hidden on snowy surfaces. This is true of:

hedgehogs
ermines
golden eagles

Female mammals have teats to nurse their young. A baby bear is called:

a cub
a kitten
a puppy

Pandas eat large quantities of bamboo. They live in China and Tibet. These areas are found in:

Europe
Asia
America

Asian and African elephants live in groups led by an older female. This female is occasionally joined by adult males for mating. One of the ancestors of the elephant is:

the dinosaur
the mammoth
the sea elephant

Hippopotamuses spend most of their time half-submerged in rivers and lakes. They are pachyderms, like elephants and rhinoceroses. Pachyderm means:

giant animal
wild animal
thick-skinned animal

Cetaceans are mammals which have completely adapted to marine life. They are sociable, move in groups, and offer each other mutual protection. Which of these three animals is a cetacean?

the whale
the crocodile
the shark

Rhinoceroses have almost become extinct, since they're hunted for a part of their body that, according to Chinese legend, could help offset the effects of age. Which part is this?

the horn
the hoof
the tail

M illions of bison used to live on the Great Plains of North America. Indians hunted them for food and used their hides to make:

teepees
totems
tomahawks

S ome animal species have become rare or extinct, often due to man's intervention. This is true of a bird from Mauritius, named the:

ibis
dodo
kiwi

The famous 17th-century French poet La Fontaine made the animals in his fables speak. Which one did he call the king of the animals, although it is known for its laziness?

the fox
the tiger
the lion

Animals give us food (honey, eggs, meat), and materials to make objects or clothes. Leather comes from the cow and wool comes from:

pigs
sheep
goats

The boar is the pig's wild ancestor. It lives in small family groups, but older males are often solitary. Females (wild sows) usually give birth to litters of 10 to 14 young. The wild ancestor of today's cattle was the:

dinosaur
mastodon
aurochs

Generally, animals with large litters don't really take care of them, while other animals care for their young for a long time. Elephants have the longest care period—the young nurse up to the age of:

6 months
4 years
10 years

Animals' senses are more or less developed, often in different ways and places than ours are. Insects smell with receptors found on their:

head
abdomen
legs

Fish live in the ocean or in rivers and lakes (they are then freshwater fish). They swim with their fins and tail, and their bodies are covered with:

scales
cartilage
hair

T he length of an animal's life depends on the abundance of food, the risk of disease, and the presence of predators. Which of these mammals lives longest?

elephant
man
lion

T he female pig can give birth to 10 piglets at the same time, which she nurses. A female pig is called a:

sow
heifer
trout

Wasps spend part of their time hunting for insects to feed to their larvae. To kill these prey, wasps use their:

stinger
nectar
wings

A bird's feeding habits can often be inferred by the shape of its beak. Thanks to its dagger-shaped beak, the heron can catch fish. Birds with short beaks, like swallows, eat:

rodents
insects
seeds

Fleas have incredibly strong hind legs, which allow them to jump quite high. A flea measures less than ⅟₁₆″ (1.5 mm), but it can jump:

more than once its height
over 100 times its height
over 20 times its height

Hedgehogs are covered by a "coat of thorns," which is quite useful protecting them from snakes and other animals. When it senses danger it:

rolls itself into a ball
closes its eyes
attacks with its spines

The chameleon is a slow animal, which makes it easy for predators to catch. It changes colors to match its environment and becomes "invisible." Another thing that makes it unique is that:

it has no eyes
it has a huge tongue
it has a corkscrew tail

At birth, the snail already carries a thin shell on its back that protects its soft body. This is also true of another mollusk:

the octopus
the shrimp
the oyster

S ome mammals find refuge underground. They are safe there to sleep and take care of their young. Badgers and foxes live in:

molehills ●
dens ■
bedlam ▲

B eavers stake out their territory by building dams on rivers. They also build lodges, using branches in the water. In order to do all of this, they cut trees with their:

tails ●
teeth ■
claws ▲

Earthworms are invertebrates. They feed on earth and small pieces of dead leaves. How many worms can there be in one acre of grass?

10 million ●
25,000 ■
2.5 million ▲

Elephant tusks are teeth (upper incisors). Small elephants have baby tusks that fall out to be replaced by the permanent adult ones. Each adult tusk can measure 10 ft. (3 m) and weigh:

220 lbs. (100 kgs) ●
44 lbs. (20 kgs) ■
1 ton ▲

A hen sits on its eggs to keep them warm, allowing the chicks to grow and develop. The hen sometimes turns the eggs over with her leg. How long does the sitting period last?

9 months
2 months
3 weeks

The herbivorous wild sheep eats any plant. During the summer, females live with their young and without the males. The male's long, spiralled horns can weigh 13 lbs. (6 kgs). Some uses for such horns include:

musical instruments
clogs
hats

G oats give much milk. Goats are raised in the poorer parts of the world, since they eat any kind of plant. The male goat is a:

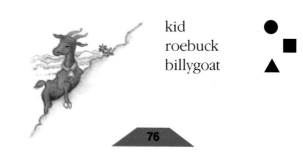

kid ●
roebuck ■
billygoat ▲

D ucks are aquatic birds that find most of their food in ponds or lakes. Domesticated geese, on the other hand, only spend time on the pond's edges. Like hens, they feed mostly on:

stale bread ●
milk ■
seeds ▲

Kangaroos are born unformed. They crawl up to the mother's pouch and finish their growth there. Like the koala, they belong to the family of:

marsupials
bears
lemurs

Some mammals, such as cows, bring swallowed foods back into their mouth to chew them again. These animals are called:

batrachians
chewers
ruminants

D oes give birth to white-spotted brown offspring. This coloration imitates sunlight in the leaves, and lets the young remain invisible. These young are called:

lambs
young boars
fawns

A ccording to the Hindu religion, killing a sacred animal is a grave crime. Which o' these three animals is sacred to them?

the dog ●
the snake ■
the cow ▲

The dog was probably the first animal to be domesticated by man. There are proofs of this domestication that date back:

10,000 years
1000 years
1 million years

The simplest classification of dogs rests on their different uses by man: watchdogs, hunting dogs, companion dogs, etc. Which of these dogs is a guard dog?

the poodle
the terrier
the mastiff

M an (*Homo sapiens*), who appeared 300,000 years ago, is a mammal classified within the order of primates. He is thought to have a common ancestor with the chimpanzee and with the:

mammoth ●

baboon ■

gorilla ▲

T he hummingbird is a bird that can fly in place, allowing it to gather the nectar from very delicate flowers. It can also fly upside down or backwards. These birds are not native to:

Europe ●

South America ■

North America ▲

The tiger's striped fur allows it to hide from its prey. It lives in Asia and, unlike other felines, it isn't a good:

swimmer
climber
runner

Dingoes, Australian wild dogs, are thought to be descended from domesticated dogs returned to the wild. There's another wild dog that lives in Africa; it's known as a:

werewolf
jackal
lynx

L ions have thick and silky manes around their necks. What other animal has a similar mane?

the giraffe
the cat
the horse

L adybugs are black with red or yellow wings marked with black spots (usually 7). These bugs are very useful to plants, since they feed on:

aphids
flowers
honey

L ike the hamster, the guinea pig is a small rodent. Guinea pigs are often raised in laboratories, because their reactions to germs or medications often resemble the reactions of man. The guinea pig is often also kept as a pet. Which other animal is kept as a pet?

shark

gerbil

elephant

M ost animals instinctively know how to swim, and keep their head out of the water. Others, like man, must learn. Another animal that must learn to swim:

monkey

kangaroo

beaver

Each animal makes a specific sound. Dogs bark, cats meow, hens cackle and horses:

roar
neigh
sneeze

Cats' eyes glow in the dark because their eyes capture and reflect any light. This adaptation allows cats to hunt at night. This trait is also true of snakes and:

owls
moles
giraffes

M ost mammals cuddle their young. Kittens express their contentment by making a motorlike sound known as:

cooing ●
purring ■
grumbling ▲

S ome animals, such as mice and squirrels, gnaw on hard foods all day to grind down their teeth, which are always growing. This is why these animals are called:

dentures ●
carnivores ■
rodents ▲

S nakes move on the ground, in water, and in trees by undulating their bodies. They can crawl on the ground because their stomachs are covered with:

wheels
scales
suction cups

T he octopus is a mollusk that moves quickly, thanks to its eight arms. These arms are also called:

squid
tentacles
sleeves

S piders use silk (which they make from their own bodies) to weave webs and trap their prey. Silkworms make cocoons in which the worms develop and change into:

caterpillars
butterflies
bees

T his mother animal is called a ewe, and its baby is called a lamb. They all live in a:

the forest
brier patch
sheepfold

During evolution, some bird species los the capacity of flight, although they stil have wings. This is true of the kakapo, a parrot, and of:

the ostrich ●

the pelican ■

the stork ▲

Eels are born in the sea and migrate towards fresh water. As adults, they return to the sea to lay eggs and die. Which fish makes the opposite trip?

pike ●

salmon ■

carp ▲

The Animal Kingdom

Invertebrates account for 95% of the earth's animals.
Vertebrates are divided into 5 large classes:

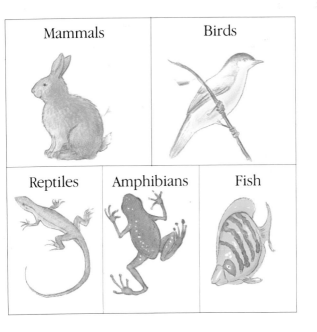

| Mammals | Birds |
| Reptiles | Amphibians | Fish |

Europe

monk seal

golden eagle

America

chinchilla

white stork

Africa

mountain gorilla

elephant

Asia

tiger

orangutan

Animal Prints

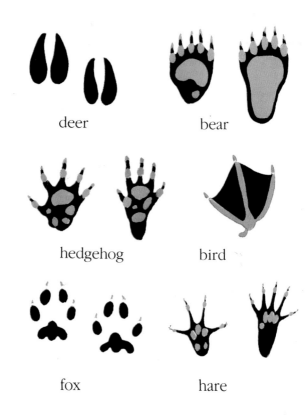

deer

bear

hedgehog

bird

fox

hare